Discovering M

Snowflakes Are Falling

by Melvin and Gilda Berger

SCHOLASTIC INC.

New York Toronto London Auckland
Sydney Mexico City New Delhi Hong Kong

ISBN-13: 978-0-545-16082-7
ISBN-10: 0-545-16082-0

12 11 10 9 8   15/0

Printed in the U.S.A. 40
First printing, January 2010

Photo Credits:

Cover: © John Block / age fotostock; Back cover: © Big Stock Photo; Title page: © Dave and Les Jacobs / Jupiter Images; page 3: © Serg Zastavkin / Shutterstock; page 4: © Masaaki Tanaka / Getty Images; page 5: © Michael Diggin / Alamy; © page 6: © Edward Kinsman / Photo Researchers, Inc.; page 7: © Big Stock Photo; page 8: © Adam Radosavljevic / iStockphoto; page 9: © ICS / Fabricius & Taylor / Grant Heilman; page 10: © StockPile Collection / Alamy; page 11: © Keith Douglas / Getty Images; page 12: © benoitb / iStockphoto; page 13: © EschCollection / Getty Images; page 14: © Joan Slatkin / Bruce Coleman Inc.; page 15: © Christopher J. Morris / Corbis; page 16: © Jose Luis Pelaez Inc. / Getty Images

BRRR! It's a cold winter day.

Snowflakes fall from the clouds.

The snowflakes fall and fall.

Can you count the snowflake's points?

Most snowflakes have six points.

What color are snowflakes?

But no two snowflakes are the same.

Falling snowflakes add up.

It's time to shovel.

More and more snowflakes fall.

Can you find
three cars in
this picture?

Cars get stuck.

What is the snowplow doing?

Here comes the snowplow!

Wind blows the snow.

Snow and wind can become a snowstorm

Look what a snowstorm can do!

Ask Yourself

1. Do snowflakes fall from clouds?
2. How many points does a snowflake have?
3. Are all snowflakes alike?
4. Why do people shovel snow?
5. What makes a snowstorm?

You can find the answers in this book.